DATE DUE

22 07 12

DEMCO

When it's hard to
eat

Judith Condon

W

FRANKLIN WATTS
LONDON·SYDNEY

First published in 1998 by
Franklin Watts,
96 Leonard Street,
London EC2A 4XD

Franklin Watts Australia,
56 O'Riordan Street,
Alexandria, Sydney,
NSW 2015

This book was created and produced
for Franklin Watts by Ruth Nason

Project management: Ruth Nason
Design: Carole Binding
Illustration: Jane Cradock-Watson
Photography: Peter Silver, Claire-Maria Cole
Consultants: Beverley Matthias/REACH
Resource Centre; staff at the British Diabetic
Association; Dr Philip Sawney;
William Sawney

Printed and bound in Belgium

ISBN 0 7496 4549 0 (pbk)

Dewey Decimal Classification 616.3

Acknowledgements
The author would like to thank all the
people featured in this book: Gary Mabbutt,
Stuart Panton, Arthur Pye, Joshua Ruddock
and family, Helen, Emma and Guy Simon,
Sarah Whiting. Also for their help and
advice: Carla Bevan, George and Olivia
Constantinides and the 1001 Supermarket,
Palmers Green, Malcolm Rant, Pamela Rant.

The photographs on pages 12, 13tl, 13cl,
13bl, 16 and 17 were taken by Claire-Maria
Cole. The photographs on the cover bl and
pages 10t, 13cr, 14 and 15t were taken by
Peter Silver. Thanks are also expressed to the
following for their permission to reproduce
photographs: John Birdsall Photography, page
7b; British Diabetic Association, page 18;
CEPHAS, pages 7t (Stockfood), 15c (John
Heinrich), 20 (Diana Mewes), 21t (Rolf
Seiffe), 24t (Stuart Boreham), 25 (Stockfood),
27 (Stockfood); Format Photographers, page
24b (Maggie Murray); Getty Images, page 19t;
Robert Harding Picture Library, page 6t;
Health Education Authority, page 6b;
MedicAlert, page 19b; Photofusion, page 11
(Paul Baldesare); Arthur Pye, page 13tr;
Science Photo Library, pages
10b (Dr P. Marazzi), 15bl
(Carl Schmidt-Luchs),
26t (Martin Dohrn), 26b
(L. Medard/Eurelios);
Steve Shott, cover br.

Contents

Introduction

We need to eat food to live. But food is also something we enjoy.

We enjoy its taste, smell and appearance. We enjoy sharing a meal with other people, particularly on special occasions.

What is your favourite thing to eat?

▲ In many parts of the world, birthdays are a time for special foods. What is your favourite party food?

fruit, vegetables, salads

starchy foods, such as bread, pasta, rice, other cereals, potatoes

meat, fish and alternatives such as eggs, nuts and lentils

foods containing fat and foods containing sugar

dairy foods, such as milk, cheese, yoghurt

A healthy diet

Some people think that a diet is just for losing weight. But 'diet' has another meaning. Your diet is the mix of all the foods you eat.

To stay healthy, you need a diet made up of a variety of foods. In this plate diagram, foods are divided into five groups. The big sections of the plate show the two food groups you should eat most from. You should eat only a little fat and sugar.

When it's hard to eat

In this book you will meet some people who need to take particular care over what they eat, in order to stay well.

Some people need to avoid certain foods which would make them ill. It can be difficult for them to know whether a meal contains these foods.

Some people need to be careful to eat regularly through the day. It is not always easy for them to stop what they are doing, in order to eat when they need to. Can you think why?

◄ The ingredients that make up this tasty pizza come from four of the five food groups. Can you name them?

► Foods from all the food groups are included in this meal.

The importance of plants

Think how much of our food and drink comes from plants.
◆ Fruit, salad, vegetables, nuts and chocolate come from plants.
◆ Cereals, such as rice and wheat, which are used to make bread and pasta, are the seeds of plants.
◆ Animals eat grass or cereals, and from animals we get eggs, milk, cheese and meat.
◆ Fish eat plankton, a tiny green plant, or they eat other fish which have eaten it!

Think about eating

Food is sometimes called the 'fuel' (like petrol in a car) that keeps our bodies going.

But food has many other purposes and meanings in our lives.

Milk is a body-building food. It makes our bones grow strong.

Glucose from the food we eat gives us energy. Glucose is made quickly from certain foods, including bananas. This is why sports players eat bananas as a healthy snack.

Bananas and fresh eggs are foods that have not been cooked before we buy them.

Giving food to someone shows that you care. It is comforting to be given something nice to eat when we are unwell.

Food may be processed in many ways, including cooking, preserving and milling (grinding).

Which of the foods in this basket have been processed?

Going out to eat gives people a chance to talk and relax. Some people like to try foods they have not eaten before. Do you?

Families spend a lot of time shopping for food, preparing meals and washing the dishes.

No one minds when a baby makes a mess at meal times, because the baby is learning. But older people are expected to have good manners.

Health problems that affect eating

▲ To avoid eating foods to which they are allergic, people check the ingredients listed on food labels.

We should all take care over what we eat, to stay well. But some people need to take particular care, because of health problems.

Some problem foods
Foods which are known to cause allergic reactions in some people include nuts, eggs, milk, cheese, prawns and wheat. A person may be allergic to one food or to several.

Food allergies

Some people react badly to certain foods. This is called being allergic, or having an allergy, to a food.

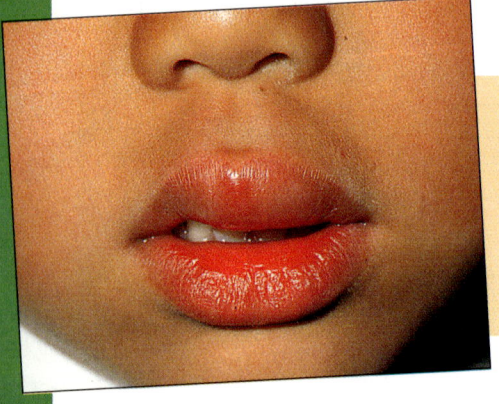

◄ Eating peanuts has made this child's mouth and lips swell.

Reactions include skin rash, tummy upsets and head aches. A severe food allergy can cause swelling of the throat, making it hard to breathe. The person may become unconscious, and even die.

No one knows why allergies happen. They tend to run in families. A child (even before it is born) may become sensitive to a certain food. Then his or her body always reacts to it.

Sometimes a great deal of 'detective work' is needed to discover which food has caused a reaction.

Diabetes

Glucose from our food is used by our body cells to make energy. After a meal, the level of glucose in our blood goes up. After we've used a lot of energy, the glucose level goes down.

Inside our bodies, an organ called the pancreas makes insulin. This controls the way our bodies store and use glucose. The process keeps our blood glucose levels fairly steady. But in people with diabetes the process does not work properly.

The two types of diabetes

In type 1 diabetes, which develops mostly before the age of 40, the pancreas stops making insulin. People with type 1 diabetes have insulin injections and eat at regular times to help keep their blood glucose levels steady.

Type 2 diabetes develops in some older people. Their bodies make too little insulin or do not use it properly. These people must take care over what they eat and may need tablets or insulin injections.

Anorexia

Some people lose the ability to judge the right amount to eat. They starve themselves, and may even die. Doctors believe this is an illness based in the mind. It seems to be connected with being unhappy, or very dissatisfied with oneself. This eating disorder is called anorexia. Another is bulimia.

Meet some people
who must take special care about eating

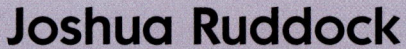

Joshua Ruddock

I am seven, and have two brothers, one sister and a dog called Sweep.

I became diabetic when I was three. The doctor says the diabetes may have started after an illness upset the way my body works.

If I follow my daily routine, I am usually all right.

I have to try to eat regularly, and that means being well organized. For instance, my mum always takes some snacks and my insulin with us when we go on a journey, in case we get held up in a traffic jam. Before swimming or football, I usually eat something with sugar in, to stop my blood glucose from dropping too low.

When I have a 'hypo', I start to feel shaky and weak. If it's bad, I feel tired and sick. Eating something sugary quickly makes me feel better again.

Joshua's daily routine:
On waking: insulin injection
Breakfast: cereal or toast
10 a.m. snack: 4 plain biscuits
Lunch: including some starchy foods
3 p.m. snack: biscuits or banana or
   2 pieces of other fruit, with milk to drink
Before dinner: insulin injection
Dinner: including some starchy foods
Before bed: cereal or toast

Joshua does a blood test to check his blood glucose level. He pricks his finger (above) and places a drop of blood on a tester (below), which gives a reading of the glucose level.

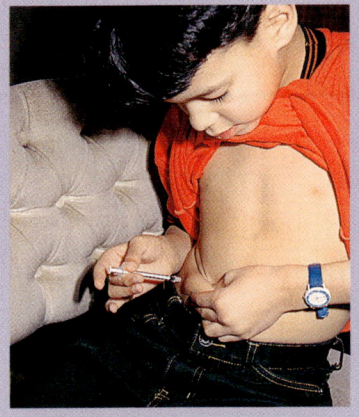

Joshua gives himself an insulin injection.

Arthur Pye

During the war, Arthur served in the Royal Army Medical Corps. Afterwards, he worked as a nurse.

Three years before he retired, Arthur began to feel tired and always thirsty. He had developed diabetes.

▲ Here is Arthur at Buckingham Palace. He received a medal from the Queen for his work as a nurse.

Now in his eighties, Arthur keeps fit by gardening, and by being careful to eat the right things.

He says: 'I used to take pills. Many older people's diabetes is controlled like that. Now I have to have insulin injections each day. You get a check-up each year at the clinic, to see what you need. It's a bit like a car's MOT!'

Meet Sarah Whiting ...

Sarah lives near the sea and works at a food factory, developing new recipes for frozen foods.

But a year before this picture was taken, she was ill with anorexia.

Sarah explains what this was like:

'I've always had a problem being very critical about myself, and feeling I was overweight. When I felt miserable, I stopped eating. I also started to exercise for four hours every day. I became so thin, it was painful to lie down. I was so weak, I couldn't open the big double doors at work.'

Sarah became so ill that she was away from work for four months. She says:

'It's as if half of your brain knows you should eat, but the other half says you mustn't.'

Speaking out

Diana, Princess of Wales, understood what it was like to have an eating problem. She described in public how feeling sad and unloved had led her to suffer from bulimia. By speaking out, she wanted to make people aware of anorexia and bulimia.

At last Sarah had support from a counsellor, who listened to her and helped her think through her problems. She became well again by eating just a little more each day.

Now Sarah is back at work, and feels much more happy and self-confident.

... and Stuart Panton

Stuart is 18 years old. He is studying science at university. He is also very good at playing the piano and the violin.

When Stuart was little he was quite poorly for some time. At about age three, he began to be nervous and irritable, and his skin became blotchy.

Soya beans are grown in the USA and China. Here are some ripe soya bean pods and some foods made from the beans.

At first his parents did not know why. Then they noticed that Stuart was worse after he had had milk, cheese or yoghurt. They realized he was allergic to all dairy foods, and to some artificial food colourings.

Instead of cow's milk, Stuart drank soya milk, and he ate porridge made with water. His parents read labels on foods very carefully to make sure the ingredients were safe for him to eat. By avoiding foods he was allergic to, Stuart got better.

Now Stuart is less allergic. However, he still does not drink much milk. He says he avoids processed food and eats mainly fresh food, which is healthier anyway.

At home

Sister and brother Emma and Guy are shown here with some of the foods they *can* eat.

Emma has coeliac disease. This means that gluten (a part of wheat, oats, barley and rye) harms her digestive system and makes her very ill. She is also allergic to chocolate, sugar and yeast. Guy is allergic to wheat, and to milk and other dairy products.

Dotty foods

In their kitchen cupboards, the foods that Emma and Guy can eat are marked with coloured dots. This means that everyone can see at a glance which foods are allowed.

Buying food

Some of the foods that Emma and Guy can eat are bought from the chemist's. For example, Emma has pasta made from flour with the gluten taken out.

Both children can eat rice, fresh meat and fish, and fruit and vegetables.

Their mother, Helen, checks the ingredients of processed foods very carefully. Did you know, for example, that most sausages contain wheat rusk and that packet ham contains milk?

Away from home

Eating away from home, at a party or in a restaurant, can be difficult for Guy and Emma. They need to know exactly what is in the food they are offered, so that they can decide if they can eat it. But sometimes friends forget, and waiters often do not know what ingredients the chef has used.

School meals

Mrs Arnold, a cook at Guy's and Emma's school, makes special lunches for them. Sometimes she uses pizza bases and sausages that they take with them.

Letting others know

If you have diabetes or a food allergy, it is important not to be shy. If you do not tell people what you need, they will not know.

Family meals

Most families are used to the fact that different people like different foods. But when one member is allergic to a common type of food, meals have to be planned with care.

A healthy meal for all

Here is Joshua (second from left), whom we met on page 12, at home with his brothers and sister. The important thing for Joshua, because of his diabetes, is to eat at regular times. He does not have to eat different foods. Starchy foods, fresh fruit and vegetables are good for all the family.

Getting together

These children are enjoying an activity holiday organized by the British Diabetic Association. The holiday organizers know about the routines of children with diabetes.

When you have a long-term health problem, it helps to know you are not the only one.

It is useful to meet others who have similar experiences and understand how you feel. You can swap ideas, support each other, and tell other people in society what you need.

Self-help

Groups of people who support each other in this way are called self-help groups. Often they begin small, in just one place. But some grow into national organizations. Some raise huge amounts of money to pay for research into particular illnesses.

Young children who have diabetes can join the Tadpole Club, run by the British Diabetic Association.

▶ H.G. Wells, one of the founders of the British Diabetic Association.

Providing a service

Some organizations provide services such as a telephone help line. They also publish magazines and books. And they try out and recommend useful products and resources.

The British Diabetic Association

The British Diabetic Association (BDA) was started in 1934 by Dr R. D. Lawrence and H.G. Wells. They both had diabetes.

Wells (1866-1946) was a famous scientist and writer of science fiction. His books include *The Time Machine* and *The Invisible Man*.

Now the BDA has more than 450 local branches for people of all ages who have diabetes and their families.

The Coeliac Society

The Coeliac Society provides a useful service to its members. Each year it publishes an up-to-date list of manufactured foods that do not contain gluten. This makes shopping much easier.

▶ Sam wears a MedicAlert bracelet. It is engraved with the information that he is allergic to peanuts.

MedicAlert

Over 4 million people worldwide belong to MedicAlert, a scheme for people with hidden medical conditions.

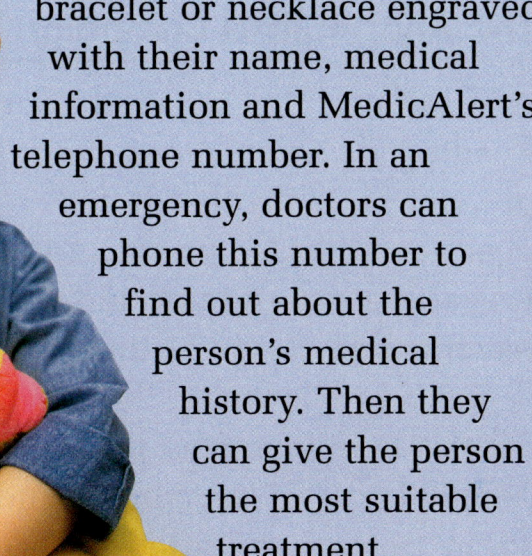

MedicAlert members wear a bracelet or necklace engraved with their name, medical information and MedicAlert's telephone number. In an emergency, doctors can phone this number to find out about the person's medical history. Then they can give the person the most suitable treatment.

Spreading the word

Some organizations and individuals work hard to inform people about health problems.

They aim to make the problems more widely understood, and to persuade the government to make laws that will be helpful. For example, a law now says that all ingredients of food products must be clearly listed for shoppers.

Anaphylaxis

Anaphylaxis is a severe, often sudden, allergic reaction. It can cause swelling in the throat, making it hard to breathe. It can cause loss of consciousness.

People with this kind of allergy must have an injection of adrenaline immediately they notice any sign of a reaction starting. They must always keep adrenaline ready with them.

▶ People who are allergic to nuts must avoid eating them. Can you name all the types of nuts shown here?

The Anaphylaxis Campaign

At a restaurant, 17-year-old Sarah Reading ate some lemon meringue pie, not knowing that it had peanuts sprinkled on top. Sarah was allergic to peanuts and her reaction was so severe that she died.

Sarah's family wanted to let other people know of the danger, and so, in 1994, they started the Anaphylaxis Campaign.

The campaign helps and advises people who have allergies, and raises money for research. It gives information to newspaper, radio and television reporters, so that they can pass on the facts to readers, listeners and viewers.

'May contain nuts'

Now shops and restaurants are more aware of the problems nuts may cause. When the same equipment is used for making several kinds of cake or icecream, it is possible for tiny traces of nut from one kind to get into another kind whose ingredients do not include nuts. Have you seen the warning on cakes or icecreams: 'This product may contain nuts'?

▲ Whole nuts are easy to spot but it is impossible to tell, by looking, if cakes contain chopped nuts, ground almonds or nut oil.

Action on eating disorders

Some people believe that the fashion industry helps to cause eating disorders such as anorexia. They say that some boys and girls try to look like fashion models they see in magazines. But these models are usually extremely thin and few people have their kind of body shape.

Some magazines have listened to this opinion. They have started to use models who are less thin.

Famous people with diabetes

Top-level sports people who have diabetes help spread the message that diabetes need not hold you back. One is Gary Mabbutt (above), who captained Tottenham Hotspur football team. Gary always checks his glucose level at half-time, to see if he needs a quick snack.

At school

Look at the posters on the walls of this school dining area. They remind the children about four of the five food groups (see page 6).

Now look at the food being eaten at each table. Have all the children chosen a good mix of foods from the different food groups? Do you remember which two groups we should eat the most from?

Why might some people need to avoid or limit some of the foods shown here?

Some children may choose only from the foods allowed by their family's religious beliefs. Some children may be vegetarians, which means that they do not eat meat.

Water is a good drink. It quenches your thirst and is provided free.
Do you know why water is good for your teeth?

Sausage rolls, crisps, sweets and biscuits are full of fat and sugar. They provide energy, but it is not healthy to eat just these foods.

Spaghetti, boiled potatoes and a baked potato are the starchy foods in these cooked meals.

The cooks wear clean aprons to protect their clothes. Is there another reason for wearing aprons? Why should cooks wear hats or keep their hair neat and short?

Spills do happen! Think of two important reasons why this mess should be cleaned up quickly.

A packed lunch of tuna fish sandwiches, yoghurt and fresh fruit provides foods from all five food groups in good balance. Can you explain how?

Chips are tasty and good for energy. But if you chose them every day, you might be filling up with too much fat.

WASH YOUR HANDS

Learning to choose

A mother's milk naturally contains all the food a new-born baby needs. But as we grow up, we are given more and more choice of things to eat.

Some people have particular choices to make because of problems with their health. But we all have a lot to learn about what is good for us. Who helps us?

▲ These children are learning to make an Indian meal.

At school

In what ways do you learn about food at school?

Schools in Glasgow run a reward scheme to encourage children to choose healthy foods for lunch. The children buy their food from the school restaurant using a charge-card, and the till keeps a record of what they buy.

For choosing fruit and vegetables they win reward points, which give them free entry to the leisure centre and swimming pool.

More information, more choice

Since your parents were children, food companies have learned to give people more information and more choice. This makes it easier for everyone, including people who have allergies or diabetes, to find healthy foods they enjoy.

- ◆ Many tinned vegetables come either with or without sugar.
- ◆ Milk can be skimmed or full-cream.
- ◆ Bread comes in many varieties.
- ◆ Some foods have reduced amounts of salt.
- ◆ Some tinned fruit is preserved in fruit juice rather than sugar syrup.

Advertising food

Makers of ready-made foods naturally want us to buy their products. These foods are wrapped in colourful packaging, given funny or exotic names, and advertised in magazines and on TV. But don't forget the wonderful fresh foods that advertise themselves, by their own appearance. Can you identify all the fruits and vegetables here?

Healthy teeth

Learning not to have sweet snacks and drinks between meals is part of learning to look after our teeth. Sugar in food and drink clings to our teeth and turns to acid, which causes teeth to decay.

How lucky we are

Remember how lucky we are to have so much to choose from. In many parts of the world children do not have a choice. They go hungry because their families are poor, or because the harvest has failed.

Words on food labels

Colourings

Fun food, such as sweets and lollies, is often highly coloured. But some children react to artificial food colourings, which may affect their mood or make them hyperactive. Look for labels that say 'No artificial colours'.

Fibre

Can you find the word 'fibre' on some food labels? Fibre helps our food move through our digestive system, and is very important for our health. Some ready-made food contains very little fibre, because processing takes the fibre out.

▲ There is lots of fibre in fruit and vegetables and in all the foods in this picture. Can you name them?

Flavour

'Flavour' on labels is misleading. Raspberry yoghurt contains real raspberries. Raspberry-flavoured yoghurt need not have any: it is made to taste of raspberries by added flavourings.

▶ These food testers are tasting food and recording their description of it on computer. The red light stops them seeing the colour of the food.

Fruit drinks

Fruit juice, squash, drink and crush often have a picture of fruit on the label, but how much fruit is inside? Juice is pure juice. Sweetened juice has added sugar. Squash contains some juice. Fruit drink and fruit crush contain least fruit of all.

Ingredients

Food labels must list the ingredients of the product in descending order of weight. This means that the first item on the list is what there is most of. The last items may be present only in very small quantities.

The ingredients in baked beans are listed: beans, tomato puree, water, sugar, salt, modified starch, onion powder, spices.

Many lollies and drinks list water as the first item.

Sugar

Fizzy drinks labelled 'diet' contain artificial sweeteners instead of sugar. People who are trying to lose weight often choose them. They are also suitable for people with diabetes.

However, some people react to artificial sweeteners and some people believe that these additives are bad for you. It is better to learn to like less sweet drinks.

Sugar can 'hide' under different names. Sometimes it may appear on labels as sucrose. Other types of sugar are fructose (naturally found in fruit) and glucose, or glucose syrup.

A safety rule

Food sold in fixed-weight packets or cans must bear a label stating its name, total weight, ingredients, and the name and address of the maker.

If anything is found to be wrong with the food, its maker can be traced, and, if necessary, all similar products made at the same factory can be withdrawn from sale.

Glossary

additives

substances added to food to alter its colour, flavour or texture, or to preserve it. There are natural additives (e.g. salt) and artificial ones (e.g. some sweeteners).

adrenaline

a hormone (a substance produced by the body) that makes the heart work faster and reduces the process that makes body tissues swell.

anaphylaxis

a very severe allergic reaction caused in some people by eating certain foods. Other causes, in other people, include bee stings and some drugs.

anorexia nervosa

an eating disorder where a person will not eat enough to keep his or her weight up to a healthy level.

bulimia nervosa

an eating disorder where a person repeatedly first eats a huge amount and then takes action (e.g. vomiting deliberately), to avoid gaining weight.

counsellor

someone trained to listen to the problems of others.

digestive system

all the parts of the body which work together to take in and use food.

gluten

a protein that is part of wheat, barley, oats and rye. In people with coeliac disease, gluten damages the lining of the digestive system.

hyperactive

nervous, restless, and unable to relax or even to sleep for long.

hypo (hypoglycaemia)

a very low level of glucose in the blood. In people with diabetes a hypo can happen if they don't have enough to eat, are very active, or have too much insulin.

MOT

a yearly test that cars over 3 years old in Britain must pass to show they are safe.

preserving

treating food to make it keep, for example by drying, freezing, or boiling it in sugar.

Stay in good shape

Food builds and repairs the body or is burned up in energy. If we eat more than we need, the extra is stored as body fat. The only way to stay a healthy weight is to balance how much you eat with how much physical exercise you do.

Useful information

Anaphylaxis Campaign,
PO Box 149, Fleet,
Hampshire GU13 9XU
tel 01252 542029

British Diabetic Association,
10 Queen Anne Street,
London W1M OBD
tel 0171 323 1531

British Nutrition Foundation,
High Holborn House,
52 -54 High Holborn,
London WC1V 6RQ
tel 0171 404 6504

Coeliac Society,
PO Box 220, High Wycombe,
Buckinghamshire HP11 2HY
tel 01494 437278

Food poisoning

Food poisoning is usually caused by eating food contaminated with bacteria or other germs. Eating food that is fresh, and has been stored and cooked correctly, is the best way to avoid food poisoning. Hands, cutlery and plates should always be spotlessly clean.

Eating Disorders Association,
1st Floor, Wensom House,
103 Prince of Wales Road,
Norwich NR1 1DW
tel 01603 619090

MedicAlert,
1 Bridge Wharf,
156 Caledonian Road,
London N1 9UU
tel 0171 833 3034

IN AUSTRALIA
Diabetes Australia,
26 Arundel Street, Glebe
tel (02) 9552 9900
Freecall 1800 451 737

Nutrition Education Services,
tel (043) 487 777

The British Nutrition Foundation publishes education packs entitled **Food – a fact of life** for pupils aged 5-11: **Stage 1** pack includes reference text for teachers, 20-minute video, question and answer data bank, wall charts, flash cards, activity sheets and workbooks. **Stage 2** pack contains teachers' manual, photographs, extended question and answer data bank, index cards, board game, two videos with teachers' notes, A4 folders of pupil activities and background information, and wallcharts. (The items are also available separately.)

A National Heart Forum teaching resource, **Eat Your Words**, is designed 'to help children think more critically about food messages and develop health-conscious attitudes'. It is available from: Broadcasting Support Services, Eat Your Words, PO Box 5, Manchester M60 3GE

Index